An introduction to British insects: a photographic

An Introduction to
British Insects
A Photographic Guide

Sally Morgan

WAYLAND

First published in Great Britain in 2006 by Wayland, an imprint of Hachette Children's Books

Hachette Children's Books
338 Euston Road, London NW1 3BH

Editor: Victoria Brooker
Senior Design Manager: Rosamund Saunders
Designer: Janis Utton

Printed and bound in China

British Library Cataloguing in Publication Data
 Morgan, Sally
   An introduction to British insects: a photographic guide
   1.Insects - Great Britain - Juvenile literature 2.Insects -
   Great Britain - Identification - Juvenile literature
   I.Title
   595.7'0941

ISBN-10: 0-7502-4848-3
ISBN-13: 978-0-7502-4848-8

Cover photograph: A peacock butterfly feeds on a dandelion.
Title page: A small tortoiseshell butterfly on a Grape Hyacinth.

Photo credits
Ecoscene: 5 (bottom), 15, 17 Ian Beames; 10, 16, 23 Rosemary Greenwood; cover and 4, 21, 22, 25, 29 (bottom) Chinch Gryniewicz; 28 Angela Hampton; 26 Bryan Knox; title page and 12 Eva Miessler; 11 Sally Morgan; 8 Lando Pescatori; 29 (top) Alastair Shay; 13, 14 Laura Sivell; 6, 7, 9, 18, 19, 20, 24, 27 Robin Williams; 5 (top) Ken Wilson. Photolibrary.com: 22.

Contents

Insects in Britain

There are many millions of different species or types of insects in the world. They range from microscopic bedbugs and fleas to giant cockroaches and dragonflies. Several hundred thousand species of insect can be found in Britain.

The best-known British insects are probably the butterflies with their large colourful wings. Ladybirds too are easy to spot. However, there are plenty of less well-known insects to discover – strange insects such as the devil's coachman, a beetle that raises up its abdomen like a scorpion, stink bugs that protect themselves by producing a horrible smell and tiny springtails in the soil that have a peg-like structure under their body to flip them into the air.

All insects have a number of features in common. Insects have three body parts, a head, thorax and abdomen. They have three pairs of legs attached to their thorax – the middle part of their body. The legs are jointed so that the insect can bend them. Most insects have two pairs of

◀ *Dandelions and other flowers attract butterflies such as this peacock butterfly.*

wings, but some only have one pair or none at all. Insects have sense organs too including a pair of compound eyes and a pair of antennae for smell and touch.

The life cycle of the insect involves metamorphosis which is a change of appearance or shape. The larva – the young of the insect – goes through metamorphosis to become an adult. Some insects have three stages in their life cycle; egg, larva and adult. The larva gradually changes, becoming more and more like the adult. Other insects, such as butterflies, have four stages; egg, larva, pupa and adult. The larva changes into a pupa and during the pupal stage the body of the larva is rearranged into that of the adult.

In this book you will read about 22 common insect species that occur across much of Britain. Most of these insects are easy to find and can be seen in parks and gardens. Some

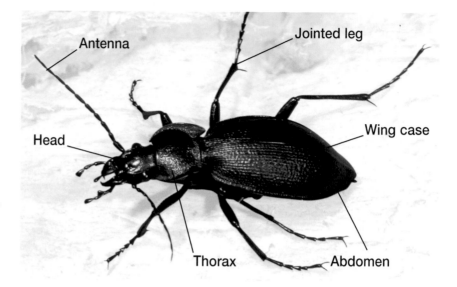

occur only in certain types of habitat, for example, you will only find dragonflies and damselflies near water. Others will be present only during a few months of the year. You will also learn about their larvae, such as caterpillars, nymphs and maggots and how to identify them.

▲ *The three body parts can be clearly seen on this beetle.*

▼ *This is the caterpillar of the elephant hawk-moth.*

Ladybird

Latin name: *Coccinella 7-punctata*
(seven-spot)

Size: about 6 mm

Time of year: April to November (ladybirds
hibernate in winter)

Habitat: gardens, parks, grasslands and
woodlands

The ladybird with its red wing cases
and black spots is one of the easiest
insects to identify. There are 41
species of ladybird living in Britain
but the most common species are the
seven-spot and the two-spot ladybirds.

The seven-spot ladybird is a small
round beetle with three and a half
spots on each of the two wing cases.
The two-spot has one large black
spot on each wing case. The bright
colours of the ladybird warn predators
such as birds that it tastes really
horrible. If a predator tries to attack

it, the ladybird produces small blobs
of bright yellow blood from its legs
as another warning.

Ladybirds are very popular with
gardeners because they eat aphids
(see page 25). Ladybirds live for about
a year and in that time they can eat
more than 5,000 aphids.

Female ladybirds lay tiny, shiny
yellow eggs in clusters on leaves in
late spring and summer. The eggs
hatch into small black larvae which
eat constantly. Ladybird larvae look
nothing like the adults. They grow to
about 13 mm long with a spiky grey-
blue skin with yellow spots. The
larvae turn into pupae from which
adult beetles emerge one to two
weeks later. In autumn, the ladybirds
look for warm, dry places to spend
the winter. Clusters of up to several
hundred can be found hiding in dry
places such as cracks in door frames,
under windowsills or under bark.

◀ *Ladybirds are
found in lots of
different habitats
such as woodland,
meadows, gardens
and hedgerows.*

Soldier beetle

◀ *Adult soldier beetles can be seen in parks and gardens from May to July.*

Latin name: *Rhagonycha fulva*

Size: up to 15 mm

Time of year: adults seen May to July

Habitat: grasslands and meadows, gardens, parks

The soldier beetle is a long, narrow beetle with an orange-red thorax and black or brown wing cases. It was named after the English soldiers of the 19th century whose uniforms were a similar colour. The red colouring is a warning to predators such as birds that soldier beetles do not taste very nice and should not been eaten.

The best time to see soldier beetles is in early summer when they can be spotted clambering over large flower heads such as cow parsley. The beetles are predators and they feed on smaller insects such as aphids and grasshopper eggs. Often they hide among flowers and wait for insects to visit. If an insect passes close by, the soldier beetle leaps out and grabs it.

The larvae of the soldier beetle are flat, dark brown to black in colour and covered in soft hairs. They have a huge pair of jaws to help them grip their prey. Their larvae are also predators. They hunt for small insects in the soil. The larvae live in the soil during the winter and in spring they pupate and become adults.

Stag beetle

Latin name: *Lucanus cervus*

Size: 50 mm

Time of year: adults fly between June and August

Habitat: woodlands

The stag beetle is Britain's largest beetle. The name 'stag' comes from the large jaws of the male beetle that look like the antlers of a stag (a male deer). Stag beetles are harmless to humans and their fearsome looking jaws are used to fight other males. The female stag beetles are smaller and they do not have these jaws.

Stag beetles have shiny brown–violet wing cases and a black thorax. From June to August they may be seen flying around on warm summer evenings. They are found mainly in the south of England. Amazingly, the adults do not eat during their short lives. Instead they survive on the fat in their body.

The female lays her eggs in rotten wood and then dies. The larvae have fat white bodies and they may spend as many as six years feeding on wood before changing into pupae. The pupae remain in the wood through the winter and the new adults emerge in spring.

▼ *The male stag beetle has huge antler-shaped jaws that it barely moves.*

Cockchafer

Latin name: *Melolontha melolontha*

Size: 25 mm

Time of year: adults fly between May and July

Habitat: gardens, parks, farmland, grasslands and woodlands

The cockchafer is often called the maybug because it is usually seen buzzing outside in May, June and July. These large beetles fly at dusk and often crash noisily into windows.

This is a heavy beetle with red-brown wing cases and legs that have spines along one side. The ends of the antennae are club-shaped, but the cockchafer can unfold the ends into a fan. This increases the surface for smelling, giving the beetles an excellent sense of smell.

The female cockchafer lays her eggs in soil. The larvae of the cockchafer have fat, creamy-white bodies and brown heads. They live in the soil for about three years. They can do a lot of damage to garden plants and crops as they feed on their roots. The larvae turn into pupae at the end of summer. During October the pupal cases split open and the adults crawl out into the soil. These adult cockchafers remain underground until the following spring when they dig themselves out of the soil and fly away.

▲ *Adult cockchafers eat leaves and flowers of many trees and shrubs but are not a serious pest, unlike their larvae.*

Peacock butterfly

Latin name: *Inachis Io*

Size: 60 mm

Time of year: April to September (adults hibernate in winter)

Habitat: gardens, parks, grasslands, hedgerows and woodlands

The peacock butterfly is one of the most common butterflies in England and Wales and is found in gardens, parks, woodlands and hedgerows. It has four large blue and red eyespots on its wings which make it very easy to identify.

The eyespots are to scare away predators such as birds and lizards. It opens its wings when threatened and flashes its 'eyes'. If this doesn't work, it opens and closes its wings rapidly and rubs them together to make a scraping noise. The undersides of its wings are dark brown and these are visible when the butterfly closes its wings making it very difficult to spot when it rests.

Female peacock butterflies lay their eggs on nettles. The caterpillars hatch and stay together in a group as they feed on nettle leaves. The caterpillars are black with small white spots. Their bodies are covered with short spines. They pupate after a few weeks and the adults appear from July onwards.

In September, the adult butterflies start to look for dark, dry places to spend the winter hibernating. These include hollow trees, crevices in walls, sheds and garages. They emerge again in spring to mate and breed. The peacock butterfly is probably the longest-lived butterfly in Britain, with the adults surviving from late July, well into the following spring, and sometimes into June.

◄ *The peacock butterfly feeds on nectar from flowers, especially buddleia and lavender.*

Large white butterfly

◄ *The large white butterfly is not popular with gardeners as the caterpillars eat crops such as cabbages and Brussels sprouts, as well as flowers such as nasturtiums.*

Latin name: *Pieris brassicae*

Size: 65 mm

Time of year: April to October (adults)

Habitat: most, especially gardens, allotments, parks and farmland

The large white butterfly is also called the cabbage white because it is a major pest of cabbages. Adult butterflies are seen from April to October in gardens, allotments, parks and other places where there are lots of flowers.

The large white butterfly has white wings with black tips on the forewings (front wings). It is easy to tell the male and female apart. The females have two black spots on each forewing while the males have no spots.

The females lay clusters of up to 100 yellowish eggs on the undersides of leaves, especially the leaves of cabbage plants. The caterpillars are grey-green and mottled with black spots and yellow stripes. They stay together, feeding on leaves. The caterpillars smell unpleasant and do not taste very nice because their bodies contain mustard oil which they get from the leaves they eat. This is a defence against predators such as birds. When they are ready to pupate, the caterpillars move to a sheltered place under a fence, on a tree trunk or in a shed. They stay as a pupa through the winter and the adults emerge in spring.

In summer the numbers of large white butterflies increase as butterflies fly across the Channel from Europe in search of food.

Small tortoiseshell butterfly

Latin name: *Aglais urticae*

Size: 50 mm

Time of year: March to September (adults)

Habitat: gardens, parks, grasslands and woodlands

The small tortoiseshell butterfly is a common sight in gardens. It gets its name from its speckled bright orange and black wings which have a row of blue spots around the edges. The undersides of the wings are dark grey and brown and are visible when the butterfly is resting. These colours blend with the ground and give camouflage.

Small tortoiseshells can be seen flying on warm spring days. The females lay a large cluster of between 80 and 200 eggs on the underside of stinging nettle leaves. The caterpillars hatch after 10 days or so. The tiny caterpillars spin a web of silk threads over the top of the nettle. They stay within this web for protection. The caterpillars are black and covered in short spines. There are two yellow lines along their sides and this warns predators that they are not good to eat. When the caterpillars are ready to pupate, between June and September, they move away and find a sheltered spot in a shed or under a fence.

In autumn, the adults look for a safe place to spend the winter and often they fly into lofts, cool rooms of houses, garages and sheds. They become active again in spring.

▼ *Small tortoiseshells visit flowers such as this Grape Hyacinth to feed on nectar. Large flowers such as the buddleia may be covered in butterflies in late summer.*

Common blue butterfly

Latin name: *Polyommatus icarus*

Size: 35 mm

Time of year: May to October (adults)

Habitat: grasslands, parks, coastal sand dunes, woodlands and heaths

Several types of blue butterfly can be found throughout Britain during the summer months. They include the silver spotted, chalkhill, holly, and adonis blue butterfly. All these butterflies are small and most of them can fly quickly. The common blue butterfly lives on grasslands, dunes, meadows, parks, woodland and heaths. The adults drink the nectar of flowers, especially the flowers of thyme and marjoram.

The upper sides of the wings of the male butterfly are pale violet-blue and they glitter in the sun. The undersides are grey and beige with spots. The female looks very different. Her upper wings are brown with orange markings.

The female lays her eggs on plants of the pea family such as clover and vetch. The caterpillars are green and furry so they are camouflaged amongst the leaves. They spend the winter resting at the base of the food plant and become active again in March. They pupate in April and the adults emerge in early summer.

▲ *The male blue butterfly is far more colourful than the female. It is easily spotted, so when it lands, it usually raises its wings so that it is not so noticeable to predators.*

Meadow brown butterfly

Latin name: *Maniola jurtina*

Size: 50 mm

Time of year: June to September (adults)

Habitat: grasslands, verges, gardens and parks

Meadow brown butterflies are common almost everywhere in Britain. They are seen near grasses in fields, at the edges of woodlands and by roads from June to September. They visit the flowers of thistles and knapweed to drink nectar. In some parts of Britain hundreds of these butterflies can be seen flying at once. Most butterflies are active on warm sunny days and they rest on overcast and rainy days. However, the meadow browns fly on dull days and may even fly in drizzle.

These butterflies are a dull brown colour with bright orange-brown patches on their wings. There is a single dark eyespot on the underside of each forewing to scare away predators such as birds. The female's wings have bright orange patches and a large eyespot. The male is smaller and darker in colour than the female and its eyespot much less noticeable.

Meadow brown butterflies can be seen flying through the summer, but individual butterflies only live for about a month, which is shorter than many other butterflies. The female butterfly lays her eggs on grasses. The caterpillars are yellowish-green with a dark line down the back and a narrow white stripe on each side. They feed on grass for about nine months and turn into pupae the following May.

▲ *The eyespots are easy to see on the wings of this resting female meadow brown butterfly.*

Hawk-moth

Latin name: *Deilephila elpenor* (elephant hawk-moth)

Size: 50 – 70 mm

Time of year: June to August (adults)

Habitat: woodland clearings, waste ground, along streams and river banks

There are 12 different species of hawk-moth found in Britain. They include the humming-bird, poplar, lime and death's head (it gets its name from the yellow pattern on its thorax which is said to look like the face of a dead person) hawk-moths. One of the most interesting is the elephant hawk-moth. Its wings, body and antennae are pink and its legs are white. The moth gets is name from the behaviour of the caterpillar. When the caterpillar is threatened the front part of its body swells up like an elephant's head (look at the photograph on page 5). This causes two eyespots to enlarge to scare away predators.

Elephant hawk-moths are found living near to willowherb, a plant that grows in woodland clearings, on waste ground and along river banks. The adults appear between June and August. They are active at dusk when they visit the flowers of the honeysuckle to sip nectar.

The females lay their eggs on leaves of the willowherb and fuchsias in the garden. The caterpillar is brown-grey in colour. In late summer the caterpillar buries itself in the soil and pupates. The pupa stays in the ground all winter and the adult moth emerges the following summer. The adults live for a few weeks.

◄ *The white legs of the elephant hawk-moth stand out against its pink wings and body.*

Burnet moth

Latin name: *Zygaena filipendulae* (six-spot)

Size: 30 mm

Time of year: June to August

Habitat: grasslands, coastal sand dunes, meadows and marshes

Most moths are active at night, but the burnet moth is one of the few moths that are active during the day. There are seven species of burnet moth, the most common of which are the six-spot and the five-spot. The only difference between these two types of burnet moth is the number of spots. The burnet moth is seen flying over grasslands, meadows and marshes from June to August. These moths are found in groups and they live in meadows and sand dunes where the bird's-foot trefoil grows. The moths visit thyme flowers to drink nectar.

Burnet moths have green-black wings with red spots. These moths are very poisonous to their predators, such as birds, as their body contains a poison called cyanide. They get this poison from the plants on which the caterpillars feed. This makes them very distasteful and predators such as birds quickly learn to leave these moths alone!

The female lays her eggs on leaves of bird's-foot trefoil. The caterpillars, which are pale yellow with black marks, feed on the leaves of this plant all summer. They spend the winter months resting at the base of the plant and become active again in spring. The adult moths emerge in summer.

▼ *The six-spot burnet moth has six red spots on each of its forewings. Its hind wings are red.*

Common wasp

◄ The common wasp has a yellow face with black markings.

Latin name: *Vespula vulgaris*

Size: 19 mm

Time of year: May to September, especially late summer

Habitat: gardens, parks, grasslands and woodlands

The yellow and black colours of the common wasp warn other animals that it has a poisonous sting. Wasps can use their sting over and over again. In late summer, wasps are attracted to sweet drinks and food and if they are disturbed by people they may sting.

The common wasp has a yellow and black head, a black and yellow thorax and a yellow abdomen with black bands. Its antennae are black and it has yellow legs. Common wasps feed on fallen fruit and nectar as well as insects which they kill with their sting. Sometimes they invade honey bees' nests to steal their honey.

Common wasps are social insects that live together in nests made from paper. There are usually about 2000 wasps in one nest. They usually build their nest in holes in the ground. The paper is made by the wasps chewing small amounts of wood taken from trees and fences. They mix this with saliva to form a pulp which is added to the nest in thin strips.

Wasps can be aggressive if their nest is disturbed. If a wasp stings an animal or a person, the poison in the sting releases a chemical. When the other wasps smell this chemical they know they are being attacked and they will sting any animal in defence.

Honey bee

Latin name: *Apis mellifera*

Size: 16 mm

Time of year: April to September

Habitat: gardens, parks, orchards, meadows and woodlands

Honey bees are a common sight in summer, flying from flower to flower in search of pollen and nectar. Their Latin name is *Apis mellifera* which means 'honey bearing'. Honey bees are found in gardens, orchards, woodland and meadows where flowers are abundant.

Honey bees have brown or black bodies with a band of orange. They have a hairy thorax and a small waist between their thorax and abdomen. They sting when threatened but unlike wasps they can only sting once and then they die.

Honey bees are social insects that live together in large colonies in a nest. Most of the bees are workers that collect food, guard the nest and look after the young. There is one queen bee which has a much longer and narrower abdomen than the workers. Her job is to lay the eggs. There are a few male drones and their only job is to fertilise the eggs that will develop into new queens.

The nest itself is made up of many cells, the walls of which are made from wax that is produced by the worker bees. The queen bee lays a single egg in each cell and the eggs hatch into larvae. The workers feed the larvae with a mixture of pollen and honey. After about four days the larvae turn into pupae and a few days later new worker bees emerge.

▲ *Worker bees collect pollen and nectar from flowers which they use to feed their larvae.*

Black garden ant

Latin name: *Lasius niger*

Size: up to 5 mm

Time of year: all year, flying ants seen July and August

Habitat: gardens, parks, grasslands, heaths and woodlands

The black garden ant is found in many places including gardens, parks grasslands, heaths and woods. They will also enter houses in search of food. Ants feed on a range of mostly sweet foods as well as small insects and seeds. They love to feed on the sugary liquid, known as honeydew, that is produced by aphids. The ants make the aphids produce honeydew by stroking them with their antennae.

Ants are social insects and they live together in huge colonies in a nest which they make in the ground. Most of the ants are workers which are wingless females that are unable to breed. They have a dull brown–black body. There are one or two queen ants in the colony that lay the eggs. A queen ant grows up to 15 mm in length and is mid brown in colour.

In July and August swarms of winged ants emerge from nests under stones. These ants are both males and females and are about twice the size of worker ants. They fly into the air and the male and females mate. After mating, the males die and females lose their wings and look for new nest sites. Many of these winged ants are eaten by predators such as birds, but a few survive to start new colonies.

◀ *The worker ants leave the nest to search for food. They follow each other along scent trails across the ground. They use this scent to find their way back to the nest.*

Common field grasshopper

Latin name: *Chorthippus brunneus*

Size: 20 mm

Time of year: May to October

Habitat: grasslands

One of the sounds of summer in the countryside is the chirping of the grasshopper. The male common field grasshopper chirps to attract females. It produces its 'song' by rubbing its hind leg, which has a row of tiny pegs, against its forewing. The song of this grasshopper consists of a series of 'sst' sounds repeated at 2 second intervals for about 12 seconds.

Common field grasshoppers appear in a range of colours from green to purple and even black. These colours provide good camouflage in grass. Their wings are narrow and they extend beyond the end of their abdomen. Grasshoppers can fly but usually they use their long hind legs to jump into the air and glide.

In late summer, the females lay their eggs in grass. The eggs are protected by a foamy covering. The eggs stay like this until spring when they hatch into nymphs (larvae). The nymphs look like adults but they do not have any wings. Grasshoppers do not go through a pupal stage. Instead the nymphs grow and get more like adults. The common field grasshopper is just one of nine species of grasshopper in Britain.

▲ *Grasshoppers live for about five months, feeding on grass.*

20

Hoverfly

Latin name: Various – there are many species of hoverfly

Size: 11 – 15 mm

Time of year: March to November

Habitat: gardens, parks, grasslands, wetlands and woodlands

Hoverflies are small insects that look just like a bee or a wasp but they do not sting. However many predators such as birds avoid them because they look like a dangerous insect that will sting.

There are about 250 different species of hoverfly in Britain and they fly between March and November.

They get their name from the way they hover in front of flowers and dart around. The adults feed on the nectar and pollen of flowers and the honeydew of aphids.

The larvae of the hoverfly are very varied and some even look like slugs!

They all feed on different foods. Some larvae eat plants while others feed on rotting wood and fungi. Many of the hoverfly larvae in the garden prey on aphids and other pests. The larvae of the drone fly, a type of hoverfly, is called a rat-tailed maggot and it lives in dirty pools of water. After a few weeks, they pupate and the adult flies emerge from the pupae and fly away.

▼ *Most hoverflies have a yellow and black body that looks like a bee or wasp. However, they do not have a narrow waist between their thorax and abdomen like a bee or wasp.*

Housefly

Latin name: *Musca domestica*

Size: 8 mm

Time of year: all year

Habitat: houses, gardens, farm buildings

Houseflies are a common sight in homes and gardens. They are found around the world where they live in houses and other buildings and near rubbish. In fact they are found anywhere where there are people.

The housefly has red eyes and a yellow-grey body with four black stripes on the thorax. They have sucking mouthparts. When they land on food they vomit up the contents of their stomach on to the food to break it down into a liquid and then they suck it up.

The female housefly lays hundreds of tiny white eggs, which soon hatch into maggots. The maggots have a yellow-white body with no legs or eyes. They feed on the food on which the eggs were laid. When they are fully grown they pupate and change into adults. In warm conditions this whole life cycle can take place in just seven to ten days. Some larvae and pupae survive the winter under manure piles or similar places. The adult flies live for between 15 and 25 days.

Houseflies can be a health hazard because they crawl all over animal dung, rubbish piles and other dirty surfaces and pick up germs. When they fly into a kitchen they carry the germs with them and transfer them onto food.

▼ *The housefly sucks up its food through its mouth part which is called a proboscis.*

Crane fly

Latin name: *Tipula paludosa*

Size: 20 mm

Time of year: July and August

Habitat: gardens, parks, grasslands

Many people are scared of crane flies, or daddy-long-legs, perhaps because these insects look a bit like large spiders and by the way they move. Crane flies are attracted by lights and during the evening they fly into rooms through open windows and flap against lampshades and other lights.

Crane flies are large flies with very long and fragile legs. They have two long, narrow wings. Their grey-brown body is long and thin too. The adults hardly feed during their short lives. Sometimes they sip nectar, but often they do not feed on anything, surviving on the fat stores in their body.

The female lays her eggs in the ground, where they hatch into larvae called leatherjackets. They get this name from the way the larvae look as if they are covered in leather. These larvae look rather like maggots and they live in the soil where they feed on the roots of plants. For this reason, they are a pest in the garden. A large number of leatherjackets can destroy a lawn. Birds, such as starlings, feed on leatherjackets and they can damage a lawn too as they stick their beak into the soil to pull out the leatherjackets.

▲ *If the crane fly is caught by a predator its long legs break off easily so they can escape. Crane flies can survive without one or two legs.*

Earwig

The curved forceps on this earwig indicate that it is a male. The earwig opens and raises its forceps when threatened.

Latin name: *Forficula auricularia*

Size: 13 mm

Time of year: all year but most likely April to November

Habitat: many, including gardens, parks, grasslands and woodlands

Earwigs are easy insects to identify because they have a pair of dangerous-looking pincers at the end of their body. Their name may have come from an old wives' tale that suggested that earwigs creep into the ears of sleeping people and burrow into their brains! However, it is more likely that they got their name from the shape of their hind wings that look like human ears and the word 'earwig' may have come from 'ear wing'.

The earwig is a glossy brown insect with a flattened and elongated body.

The male earwig has a pair of very long and curved pincers while those of the female are smaller and straight. Although earwigs have two pairs of wings, they do not fly very often, preferring to run along the ground.

Earwigs are mostly nocturnal insects, coming out at night to feed. During the day they hide in dark places, such as under pots and in flowers. They are mainly scavengers, feeding on dead leaves, flowers, small insects and the bodies of dead animals. They particularly like to eat the petals of chrysanthemum and dahlia flowers.

Female earwigs are unusual because they care for their eggs and young. The female lays 20 to 30 eggs which she looks after through the winter. When the young hatch, she cares for them until they are able to look after themselves. The young look like small adults except they have no wings.

Aphid

Latin name: *Macrosiphum rosae*
(rose aphid)

Size: 2 – 3 mm

Time of year: April to October

Habitat: gardens, parks, grasslands,
farmland and woodlands

The aphid goes by several different names including blackfly, greenfly and plant lice. There are more than 500 different types of aphid in Britain and a number of them are garden pests.

An aphid has a pear-shaped body that is just a few millimetres in length. Its colour ranges from black to pink, though most are green. Its pair of antennae are particularly long. It lives in large groups that form clusters around plant stems, leaves and flower buds, especially those of broad beans and roses. In summer, most aphids are wingless females.

Aphids are sucking insects and they can do a lot of damage to a plant. They have long, thin biting mouthparts that they can insert right into the stem of a plant and suck out the sap. The sap is rich in sugar and provides the aphid with all its food. Aphids take in so much sugar that they have to get rid of some of it as honeydew. The honeydew attracts ants that love to feed on it.

In spring, the eggs of aphids laid the previous autumn hatch into wingless females. These females have a special ability to produce live young without mating. All their offspring are females. The numbers of female aphids increase greatly during the summer. In autumn, both male and female aphids are born. They mate and the female lays the eggs that will hatch in spring.

▼ *Aphids suck sap from plant stems and harm the plant.*

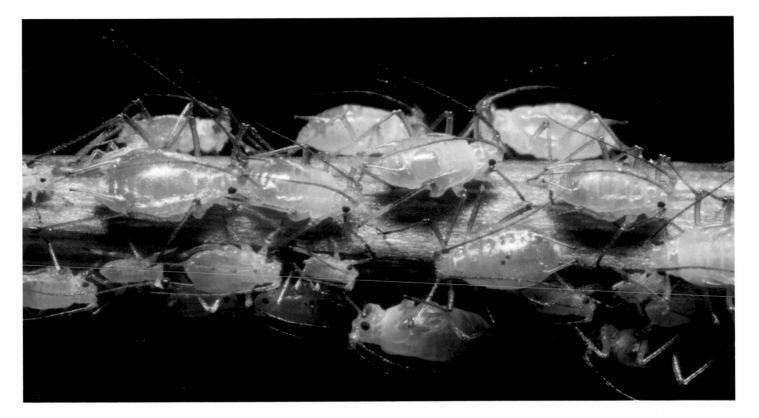

Emperor dragonfly

Latin name: *Anax imperator*

Size: 100 mm (wingspan)

Time of year: adults between June and August

Habitat: ponds, lakes, rivers

The emperor dragonfly is one of the fastest flying insects. Its excellent eyesight and its fast flight make the dragonfly a fearsome hunter. In summer, emperor dragonflies can be seen flying up and down streams and rivers, lakes and ponds hunting for prey. Their huge eyes can detect prey up to 15 m away.

The adult dragonfly is able to catch most of its insect prey while it is flying, grabbing the insects with its legs. It eats small insects while it is flying but it takes larger prey to a resting perch.

The male has a brilliant blue-green body with a central black stripe. Its large head is green. The female is slightly shorter with a greenish body that ends in a brown tip.

The female lays her eggs in water and they hatch into larvae called nymphs. Nymphs spend the next two years in water, gradually getting larger. They are predators too. The nymph has extendable jaws that end in deadly hooks, which it uses to catch and kill animals such as tadpoles and small fish. When a nymph crawls out of the water, its skin splits and a new adult emerges. The dragonfly dries its wings and then flies away.

◀ *Dragonflies rest with their wings spread open.*

Banded demoiselle damselfly

Latin name: *Calopteryx splendens*

Size: 60 mm

Time of year: May to August

Habitat: fast flowing streams

Damselflies are related to dragonflies but they have a weaker, fluttering flight and a more delicate body. When they rest, most damselflies raise their wings above their body like a butterfly. There are a number of types of damselfly in Britain and the largest is the banded demoiselle.

Banded demoiselle damselflies are found near fast flowing streams in England and Wales from May to the end of August. They feed on insects which they catch while they are flying. The male has a shiny green body and each of its four wings has a patch of blue. The female has a green body and wings.

The female lays her eggs in water. After about two weeks they hatch into nymphs. The nymphs live in the water for two years feeding on small animals. Damselfly nymphs look at bit like dragonfly nymphs except they have three feather-like structures that stick out the end of the abdomen for obtaining oxygen from the water. In early summer, they crawl out of the water and within hours become adults.

▲ *This is a male banded demoiselle damselfly with patches of blue on its wings.*

Be an insect detective

You can become an insect detective. First, you will need some equipment. Take this book with you to help you to locate and identify the insects that you find. You will also need a notebook, pencil, magnifying glass and a small clear plastic pot with a lid in which you place some of the insects you find. A digital camera can be useful for recording the insects that you find. You can catch the insects in different ways, for example using a butterfly net, with a piece of equipment called a pooter that you use to suck insects into a container. Or simply use a small paint brush to catch the insect and pop it into your collecting pot. You can look at the insects more closely with the magnifying glass once they are in the pot.

The best place to start looking for insects is in a garden or local park. A nettle patch is often home to many different insects (be careful to avoid being stung) and in summer you may find lots of caterpillars. When you find butterflies watch them for a few minutes to see which plants they visit. You may spot them laying their eggs. Rotting logs can be a good place for insects too, especially beetles. Have a look under the logs, but remember to put the logs back. Have a look in a vegetable garden or allotment for large white caterpillars eating cabbage

◀ *This girl is looking at insects that have been sucked into a container using a pooter.*

leaves! Different types of insects including dragonflies and damselflies can be seen flying near ponds. Most moths come out at night. It's surprising just how many moths can be attracted to a torch light shone on a white sheet on a washing line.

It is a good idea to record your discoveries in your notebook. You can record all sorts of information such as where and when you found the insect, what it was doing, the plants it visited and so on. If the insect stays around long enough you may be able to make a quick sketch or take a photograph of it. This can be useful if you are not quite sure what type of insect it is. Make sure you make a note of features such as the number and colour of its wings, the length and shape of its antennae and the colours of its body.

▲ *If you sit beside a patch of flowers in the sun you can watch insects, such as bumble bees, at work.*

◀ *Lots of insects can be found among garden plants. These aphids were hidden from sight under a leaf.*

Glossary

Abdomen The back part of an insect, joined to the thorax.

Antennae An insect's feelers, its sense organ for smell and touch.

Camouflage Colours on an animal's body that blend with the background, making the animal difficult to spot.

Caterpillar The larva of a butterfly or moth.

Compound eyes Large eyes of an insect made of lots of units which work together.

Drone A male bee whose role is to mate with the queen bee.

Forceps Part of an insect's body shaped like a pair of pincers.

Larva The young of an insect that hatches from an egg.

Maggot The larva of a fly.

Metamorphosis The change in shape or appearance as a larva changes into an adult insect.

Nectar The sugary liquid produced by some flowers.

Nocturnal To be active at night.

Nymph The larva of an insect such as a dragonfly or a damselfly.

Poisonous When something contains a harmful substance.

Pollen The yellow dust-like specks produced by the male parts of flowers.

Predator An animal that hunts and eats other animals.

Prey An animal that is hunted and eaten by another animal.

Proboscis The long, thin mouthpart of an insect, used to suck up nectar.

Pupa The third stage in the life cycle of some insects. For example, butterflies have four stages: egg, larva, pupa and adult. *Plural: pupae.*

Pupate To turn into a pupa.

Scavenger Animal that feeds on the dead remains of plants and animals.

Thorax The middle part of the body of an insect. The legs and wings are attached to the thorax.

Vomit To be sick.

Further information

Books

Field Guide to the Insects of Britain and Northern Europe by Michael Chinery (Collins, 1993)

Butterflies of Britain and Europe by Tom Tolman, Richard Lewington (Illustrator) (Collins, 2004)

The Colour Identification Guide to the Caterpillars of the British Isles by Jim Porter (Viking, 1997)

Pocket Guide to the Butterflies of Great Britain and Ireland by Richard Lewington (British Wildlife Publishing, 2003)

The Wildlife Trust's Guide to Butterflies and Moths illustrated by Stuart Carter (New Holland, 2002)

The Wildlife Trust's Guide to Insects illustrated by Sandra Doyle and Stuart Carter (New Holland Publishers, 2002)

Minibeasts: Beetles by Claire Llewellyn (Franklin Watts, 2004)

Animal Kingdom: Arthropods by Ruth Miller (Harcourt Raintree 2005)

Websites

http://www.rspb.org.uk/gardens/guide/atoz/i/insects.asp
Looks at the A to Z of a wildlife garden including many different British insects.

http://www.butterfly-conservation.org/index.shtml
A charity set up to protect British butterflies and their habitats.

http://www.nhm.ac.uk/nature-online/life/insects-spiders/
The Natural History Museum website looks at everything from butterfly conservation to edible insects.

Places to visit

The Natural History Museum, Cromwell Road, London SW7 5BD
Visit the Creepy Crawlies live gallery and find out more about thousands of insects from around the world.

Butterfly and Insect World, Dobbies Garden World, Lasswade, Midlothian, Edinburgh EH18 1AZ
Discover butterflies and insects found all over the world.

Look out for nature reserves and bug houses near where you live.

The website addresses (URLs) included in this book were valid at the time of going to press. However, because of the nature of the Internet, it is possible that some addresses may have changed, or sites may have changed or closed down since publication. While the author and publisher regret any inconvenience this may cause the readers, no responsibility for any such changes can be accepted by either the author or the publisher.

Index

Page numbers in **bold** indicate pictures.